Tech-Savvy Students Mastering Assessment with Technology

Rodin

TABLE OF CONTENTS

Chapter 1: Introduction to Technology-based Assessment Tools

The Importance of Assessment in Education

Assessment plays a crucial role in education, as it helps students and educators gauge progress, identify areas for improvement, and make informed decisions. In today's digital age, technology has become an invaluable tool for enhancing the assessment process, allowing students to become tech-savvy learners. In this subchapter, we will explore the significance of assessment in education and how technology can be harnessed to master assessment.

Assessment serves various purposes in education. Firstly, it provides valuable feedback to students, enabling them to understand their strengths and weaknesses. By identifying areas of improvement, students can take necessary steps to enhance their learning experience. Additionally, assessment helps educators evaluate the effectiveness of their teaching methods and modify their strategies accordingly. It also assists in measuring the attainment of learning objectives and standards, ensuring that students are meeting the required benchmarks.

With the advent of technology, assessment practices have evolved significantly. The integration of technology in assessment not only makes the process more efficient but also enhances student engagement and motivation. One of the key benefits of utilizing technology in assessment is the ability to provide immediate feedback. Through online quizzes and interactive platforms, students can receive instant feedback on their performance, enabling them to reflect on their mistakes and rectify them promptly.

Moreover, technology offers a wide range of assessment tools that cater to different learning styles. From multimedia presentations to online portfolios, students can demonstrate their understanding in creative and innovative ways. This not only enhances critical thinking and problem-solving skills but also encourages self-expression and creativity.

Furthermore, technology allows for the collection and analysis of data, enabling educators to make data-driven decisions. By analyzing assessment data, teachers can identify patterns and trends, which can inform instructional strategies and interventions. This ensures that students receive personalized and targeted support, leading to improved learning outcomes.

In conclusion, assessment is an indispensable aspect of education, and technology has revolutionized the way it is conducted. By embracing technology, students can become tech-savvy learners, benefiting from immediate feedback, personalized assessments, and data-driven instruction. As technology continues to advance, it is crucial for students to master assessment with technology, equipping themselves with the necessary skills for success in the digital age.

Advantages of Technology-based Assessment Tools

In this era of rapid technological advancements, the field of education has also witnessed a significant transformation. The traditional methods of assessment and evaluation have been replaced with innovative and efficient technology-based assessment tools. These tools offer numerous advantages to students, making the learning experience more engaging, personalized, and effective.

One of the key advantages of technology-based assessment tools is their ability to provide immediate feedback. Unlike traditional methods where students have to wait for days or even weeks to receive their grades, technology-based tools generate instant feedback. This allows students to identify their strengths and weaknesses in real-time and make necessary adjustments to improve their performance. Immediate feedback also promotes a sense of autonomy and responsibility among students, enabling them to take charge of their learning journey.

Another advantage is the flexibility that technology-based assessment tools offer. These tools can be accessed at any time and from any location, providing students with the convenience of studying and evaluating their progress according to their schedule. This flexibility also allows students to revisit previous assessments and track their growth over time, facilitating a deeper understanding of the subject matter.

Additionally, technology-based assessment tools promote active learning. These tools often incorporate interactive features such as multimedia elements, simulations, and gamification, which enhance student engagement and motivation. By making the assessment process more interactive and enjoyable, technology-based tools encourage students to actively participate in their own learning, leading to better retention and comprehension of the material.

Furthermore, technology-based assessment tools enable educators to tailor assessments according to individual student needs. Through the use of data analytics and machine learning algorithms, these tools can adapt to the learning pace and style of each student. This personalized approach ensures that students receive assessments that align with their abilities and challenges, fostering a more efficient and effective learning experience.

In conclusion, technology-based assessment tools have revolutionized the field of education by offering numerous advantages to students. From immediate feedback and flexibility to promoting active learning and personalization, these tools empower students to take ownership of their education and enhance their overall academic performance. Embracing technology-based assessment tools will undoubtedly equip students with the necessary skills and knowledge to thrive in the digital age.

Challenges in Traditional Assessment Methods

Assessment and evaluation play a crucial role in education, helping both teachers and students gauge their progress and understanding. However, traditional assessment methods often present challenges that can hinder the learning process and limit the effectiveness of evaluation. In this subchapter, we will explore some of the key challenges associated with traditional assessment methods and how technology can help overcome them, specifically targeting the tech-savvy students of today.

One of the primary challenges with traditional assessment methods is their limited scope. Traditional assessments, such as written exams or multiple-choice tests, often focus on memorization and regurgitation of information rather than critical thinking and problem-solving skills. This approach can discourage students from delving deeper into the subject matter and inhibit their ability to apply knowledge to real-world scenarios. Technology offers a solution by providing platforms and tools that encourage interactive and engaging assessments, allowing students to showcase their understanding through multimedia presentations, simulations, and collaborative projects. This shift from passive to active assessment methods enables students to demonstrate their skills in a more comprehensive and authentic manner.

Another challenge of traditional assessment methods is their one-size-fits-all approach. Every student has unique learning styles, strengths, and weaknesses, which may not be accurately measured through standardized tests. This can result in unfair evaluations and limited opportunities for students to showcase their full potential. Technology can address this challenge by offering adaptive assessment tools that adapt to individual student needs, providing personalized feedback and tailored learning experiences. By leveraging technology, students can engage in self-paced learning, receive targeted support, and demonstrate their understanding in a way that aligns with their specific learning preferences.

Additionally, traditional assessment methods often lack timely feedback, which is essential for students to track their progress and make necessary improvements. Waiting for weeks to receive grades or feedback can be frustrating and discouraging, especially for tech-savvy students accustomed to instant information access. Technology can bridge this gap by enabling real-time feedback and assessment through online platforms, allowing students to receive immediate feedback on their work and make timely adjustments. This promotes a continuous learning cycle and empowers students to take ownership of their learning journey.

In conclusion, traditional assessment methods present several challenges that can impede the learning process and limit accurate evaluation. However, with the integration of technology, these challenges can be overcome, providing students with more interactive, personalized, and timely assessments. By embracing digital tools and platforms, tech-savvy students can enhance their learning experience, demonstrate their understanding in a more comprehensive manner, and receive immediate feedback to continuously improve.

Overview of the Book

"Tech-Savvy Students: Mastering Assessment with Technology" is a comprehensive guide that aims to equip students with the necessary skills and knowledge to excel in assessment and evaluation using technology. In today's digital age, technology has become an integral part of our lives, and this book recognizes the importance of harnessing its potential to enhance learning and assessment outcomes.

This subchapter provides an overview of the book, giving students a glimpse into the valuable insights and strategies they will gain as they progress through its pages. The book is specifically tailored for students in the field of assessment and evaluation in education, who are interested in leveraging technology to optimize their learning experience and improve their assessment performance.

The content of this book is divided into various sections, each focusing on a specific aspect of assessment and evaluation. The authors have carefully curated a collection of practical tips, techniques, and case studies that illustrate how technology can be effectively utilized to enhance learning and assessment outcomes.

Throughout the book, students will be introduced to a wide range of technological tools and platforms that can be integrated into their assessment practices. From online quizzes and interactive presentations to digital portfolios and data analysis technologies, the book covers various cutting-edge tools that can revolutionize the way students approach assessment. Additionally, the authors provide step-by-step instructions and troubleshooting tips to ensure students can confidently implement these technologies in their own academic journey.

Moreover, the book also delves into the importance of digital literacy and responsible technology use. Students will learn about the ethical considerations associated with utilizing technology in assessment, as well as how to navigate potential challenges and pitfalls that may arise in a digital learning environment.

By the end of this book, students will have developed a solid foundation in using technology for assessment purposes. They will be equipped with the skills and knowledge to effectively utilize technology tools in their coursework, projects, and exams, ultimately enhancing their academic performance and preparing them for success in the assessment and evaluation field.

"Tech-Savvy Students: Mastering Assessment with Technology" is an indispensable resource for students looking to optimize their learning experience, improve their assessment outcomes, and become proficient in utilizing technology for assessment purposes.

Chapter 2: Understanding Technology-based Assessment Tools

Definition and Types of Technology-based Assessment Tools

In today's digital age, technology has become an integral part of our daily lives, transforming the way we work, communicate, and learn. As students, you are likely to be tech-savvy and accustomed to using various technological tools to enhance your educational experience. One area where technology has particularly made its mark is in assessment and evaluation in education. In this subchapter, we will explore the definition and types of technology-based assessment tools, which can revolutionize the way you are assessed in your academic journey.

Technology-based assessment tools can be defined as any software or application that facilitates the evaluation of student learning outcomes through the use of technology. These tools go beyond traditional paper-based tests and offer a range of interactive and engaging features. By leveraging technology, educators can create more dynamic and personalized assessments that cater to individual student needs.

One type of technology-based assessment tool is online quizzes and exams. These tools allow students to take tests remotely, at their own convenience, eliminating the need for physical exam halls. Online quizzes can be designed with various question types, such as multiple-choice, fill-in-the-blank, and matching, providing immediate feedback to students and allowing for instant grading. This enables students to assess their understanding of the subject matter and identify areas for improvement.

Another type of technology-based assessment tool is the use of digital portfolios. These platforms allow students to showcase their work and progress over time. Through the use of multimedia elements such as videos, images, and documents, students can demonstrate their learning in a more creative and comprehensive manner. Digital portfolios also enable educators to provide personalized feedback and track students' growth and development.

Simulations and virtual reality (VR) are also emerging as powerful technology-based assessment tools. These tools provide students with immersive and realistic experiences, allowing them to apply their knowledge and skills in authentic situations. Simulations can be used to assess problem-solving abilities, critical thinking, and decision-making skills. VR, on the other hand, creates a virtual environment where students can explore and interact with content, making the learning process more engaging and memorable.

In conclusion, technology-based assessment tools offer exciting possibilities for students in the field of assessment and evaluation in education. These tools provide flexibility, interactivity, and personalization, allowing for a more comprehensive and accurate evaluation of student learning outcomes. By embracing these tools, students can take charge of their own learning, track their progress, and develop a deeper understanding of the subjects they study. As you navigate through your academic journey, keep an open mind and embrace the opportunities that technology-based assessment tools present.

Benefits of Using Technology in Assessments

In today's digital age, technology has become an integral part of our lives, transforming the way we learn, communicate, and assess our knowledge. As students, you are constantly exposed to various technological advancements that have revolutionized education. In this subchapter, we will explore the numerous benefits of using technology in assessments, and how it can enhance your learning experience.

One of the primary advantages of incorporating technology in assessments is the ability to provide immediate feedback. Traditional assessment methods, such as pen-and-paper tests, often require lengthy grading processes, leaving students waiting anxiously for their results. However, with technology-based assessments, feedback can be generated instantly, allowing you to identify your strengths and weaknesses promptly. This real-time feedback empowers you to make necessary adjustments in your learning strategies, ultimately improving your performance in subsequent assessments.

Furthermore, technology-based assessments offer a more personalized learning experience. Adaptive assessment platforms can tailor questions and content based on your individual knowledge level, ensuring that you are challenged appropriately. This personalized approach not only keeps you engaged but also helps you focus on areas that require more attention. By targeting your specific needs, technology enables you to make the most of your study time and maximize your learning potential.

Another significant benefit of using technology in assessments is the ability to access resources beyond traditional textbooks. Online platforms, educational websites, and digital libraries provide a vast range of materials, such as interactive videos, simulations, and multimedia content. These resources offer a dynamic and engaging learning experience, making complex concepts more accessible and enjoyable to grasp. Additionally, technology enables you to access these resources anytime, anywhere, promoting independent and self-paced learning.

Moreover, technology-based assessments foster collaboration and communication among students. Online discussion forums, virtual classrooms, and collaborative tools allow you to interact with your peers, exchange ideas, and seek help when needed. This collaborative learning environment not only enhances your understanding of the subject matter but also cultivates essential skills such as critical thinking, problem-solving, and effective communication.

Lastly, technology-based assessments prepare you for the digital world and the workforce of the future. As technology continues to advance and shape various industries, proficiency in digital literacy has become a sought-after skill. By engaging in technology-based assessments, you are developing essential technological skills that are highly valued in today's job market. From data analysis to online collaboration, these skills will not only benefit you academically but also provide a competitive edge in your future career endeavors.

In conclusion, the benefits of using technology in assessments are vast and transformative. From immediate feedback to personalized learning experiences, access to a wide range of resources, fostering collaboration, and preparing for the digital world, technology enhances your educational journey. Embracing technology-based assessments will not only help you succeed academically but also equip you with the necessary skills for a future driven by technology.

Commonly Used Technology-based Assessment Tools

In today's digital age, technology is integrated into almost every aspect of our lives, including education. As students, you are no strangers to the use of technology in the classroom. From interactive whiteboards to online learning platforms, technology has revolutionized the way you learn and engage with educational content. One area where technology has made a significant impact is in assessment and evaluation. In this subchapter, we will explore commonly used technology-based assessment tools that can enhance your learning experience and help you excel in your studies.

1. Online Quizzes and Tests: Gone are the days of paper and pencil tests. Online quizzes and tests allow for immediate feedback and provide a more interactive and engaging experience. These assessments can be taken from anywhere with an internet connection, providing flexibility and convenience for students.

2. Digital Portfolios: Digital portfolios are a creative way to showcase your work and progress over time. With the use of multimedia elements such as videos, images, and audio recordings, you can present your projects and assignments in a visually appealing and comprehensive manner.

3. Video Assessments: Video assessments allow you to demonstrate your understanding of a topic or concept through video presentations. This tool encourages creativity and critical thinking skills while also promoting effective communication and presentation skills.

4. Online Discussion Forums: Online discussion forums provide a space for students to engage in meaningful discussions and collaborate with their peers. These platforms allow for asynchronous

communication, ensuring that everyone has an opportunity to contribute to the conversation.

5. Simulations and Virtual Labs: Simulations and virtual labs offer hands-on learning experiences in a digital environment. These tools allow you to practice skills and conduct experiments in a safe and controlled setting, promoting active learning and problem-solving abilities.

6. Interactive Presentations: Interactive presentations, such as Prezi or PowerPoint, enable you to create dynamic and engaging presentations that go beyond the traditional slide format. With features like embedded videos, hyperlinks, and interactive elements, you can captivate your audience and deliver your message effectively.

By leveraging these commonly used technology-based assessment tools, you can enhance your learning experience and demonstrate your knowledge and skills in a more engaging and comprehensive manner. These tools not only provide immediate feedback but also foster creativity, critical thinking, and collaboration – all essential skills for success in today's digital world. Embrace the opportunities technology offers and become a tech-savvy student who masters assessment with technology.

Considerations when Choosing Technology-based Assessment Tools

In today's digital age, technology has revolutionized the way we learn and assess our knowledge. As students in a world driven by technology, it is crucial to understand the considerations when choosing technology-based assessment tools. This subchapter will delve into the key factors you should consider to make informed decisions when selecting assessment tools.

Firstly, it is important to assess the compatibility of the tool with your learning style and preferences. Each student is unique and has different approaches to learning and assessment. Some may prefer interactive multimedia tools, while others may prefer online quizzes or virtual simulations. Reflect on your learning style and select a tool that aligns with your preferences, as it will enhance your engagement and motivation.

Secondly, consider the reliability and validity of the assessment tool. Reliability refers to the consistency of the tool in measuring what it intends to measure. Validity, on the other hand, refers to the accuracy of the assessment in measuring the desired learning outcomes. Look for tools that have been extensively tested and validated, ensuring that the results obtained reflect your true understanding and abilities.

Additionally, consider the accessibility and ease of use of the assessment tool. Accessibility is crucial to ensure that all students, regardless of their physical or learning abilities, can use the tool effectively. Look for tools that provide options for customization, such as font size or color contrast, to accommodate individual needs. Furthermore, choose tools that are intuitive and user-friendly, as complex interfaces may hinder your ability to focus on the assessment itself.

Another important consideration is the support and resources provided by the tool's developer. Assessments may be challenging, and it is essential to have access to support when needed. Look for tools that offer comprehensive user guides, tutorials, and technical support. Additionally, seek tools that provide opportunities for collaboration and discussion with peers, as this can enhance your learning experience.

Lastly, consider the security and privacy measures implemented by the assessment tool. Protecting your personal information and ensuring the confidentiality of your assessment results is of utmost importance. Look for tools that adhere to data protection regulations, and inquire about how your data will be stored and used.

In conclusion, choosing the right technology-based assessment tool is crucial for enhancing your learning experience and accurately measuring your progress. Consider your learning style, reliability, accessibility, ease of use, support, and security when making your selection. By making informed decisions, you can leverage technology to master assessment and excel in your educational journey.

Chapter 3: Preparing for Technology-based Assessments

Setting Up Your Device for Assessments

In today's digital age, technology has become an integral part of our lives, including the field of education. As students, it is essential to leverage the power of technology to enhance our learning experience. One crucial aspect of this is setting up our devices for assessments. Whether you're taking online exams, quizzes, or participating in virtual assessments, ensuring that your device is ready is vital for a smooth and successful evaluation process.

First and foremost, it is crucial to have a reliable and up-to-date device. Make sure your laptop, tablet, or smartphone has the required software and hardware specifications to run the assessment platform smoothly. Check for any updates and install them before the assessment to avoid any technical glitches. It is also advisable to have a backup device available in case of any unforeseen issues.

Next, familiarize yourself with the assessment platform. Take the time to explore its features and functionalities so that you can navigate through it effortlessly during the evaluation. If there are any tutorials or user guides available, make sure to go through them to gain a better understanding of the platform's capabilities. Understanding the assessment platform will not only save you time but also allow you to focus more on the content rather than struggling with the technology.

Ensure a stable internet connection. A slow or unreliable internet connection can be a major hindrance during assessments. To avoid this, connect to a high-speed network and avoid sharing it with other bandwidth-consuming activities. If possible, use a wired connection instead of relying solely on Wi-Fi, as it tends to be more stable.

Taking care of your device's battery life is also crucial. Charge your device fully before the assessment and consider keeping the charger nearby, just in case. Running out of battery during an assessment can be a stressful situation, so taking necessary precautions will help you stay focused and avoid any interruptions.

Lastly, organize your digital files and folders. Make sure all the required materials, such as study guides, notes, and reference materials, are easily accessible on your device. Create a dedicated folder for the assessment, ensuring that all relevant files are stored in a logical and organized manner. This will save you time and minimize distractions during the evaluation.

By setting up your device for assessments, you are proactively eliminating potential technical difficulties and ensuring a smooth evaluation process. Embracing technology in assessments can significantly enhance your learning experience and help you showcase your knowledge effectively. So, take the time to prepare your device, familiarize yourself with the assessment platform, and create a conducive digital environment for success.

Familiarizing Yourself with Assessment Platforms

In today's digital age, technology has become an integral part of our lives, transforming the way we learn, communicate, and even assess our knowledge and skills. As students, it is crucial to familiarize ourselves with assessment platforms that can enhance our learning experience and enable us to showcase our abilities effectively. This subchapter aims to introduce you to the world of assessment platforms and help you understand their importance in the field of education.

Assessment platforms are online tools or software designed to facilitate the evaluation of student performance. They provide a structured and efficient way to measure your understanding of various subjects, track your progress, and receive feedback from instructors. These platforms offer a wide range of assessment methods, including quizzes, tests, assignments, and projects, allowing you to demonstrate your knowledge in different formats.

One of the significant advantages of assessment platforms is their accessibility. Whether you're studying from home or on the go, these platforms can be accessed from any device with an internet connection. This flexibility enables you to complete assessments at your own pace and convenience, eliminating the constraints of traditional paper-based exams.

Moreover, assessment platforms often incorporate interactive features that make the learning process engaging and enjoyable. They may include multimedia elements, such as videos, images, and audio recordings, to supplement the assessment content and enhance comprehension. Additionally, some platforms incorporate gamification elements, turning assessments into interactive games that motivate and challenge you to excel.

By utilizing assessment platforms, you can also benefit from immediate feedback. Unlike traditional assessment methods, which may take days or weeks to receive feedback, online platforms provide instant results and detailed analysis of your performance. This feedback allows you to identify your strengths and areas for improvement, enabling you to focus your efforts on enhancing your understanding and skills.

Furthermore, assessment platforms often offer personalized learning experiences tailored to your individual needs. They can generate customized study plans based on your performance, recommending specific learning resources and activities to address your weaknesses. This personalized approach ensures that you receive targeted support to maximize your learning potential.

In conclusion, assessment platforms have revolutionized the way we evaluate and demonstrate our knowledge and skills. By familiarizing yourself with these platforms, you can harness the power of technology to enhance your learning experience, receive immediate feedback, and access personalized resources. Embracing assessment platforms will empower you to become a tech-savvy student and master assessment with ease.

Understanding the Assessment Process

Assessment plays a crucial role in education, allowing students and teachers to gauge progress, identify strengths and weaknesses, and make informed decisions about learning strategies. In today's digital age, technology has significantly transformed the assessment process, providing students with innovative tools and opportunities to showcase their skills. This subchapter aims to provide tech-savvy students with a comprehensive understanding of the assessment process, highlighting the benefits of incorporating technology into evaluation practices.

Firstly, it is important to understand the purpose of assessment. Assessments are not merely tests or exams; they encompass a wide range of methods designed to measure knowledge, skills, and understanding. They can take the form of quizzes, projects, presentations, or even online discussions. By engaging in assessments, students can demonstrate their learning achievements and receive valuable feedback from teachers and peers.

Technology has revolutionized assessment practices, offering students exciting opportunities to showcase their abilities. Digital platforms and applications allow for interactive and multimedia-rich assessments that go beyond traditional paper-based exams. For instance, students can create videos, podcasts, or digital portfolios to present their knowledge and skills in a more engaging and personalized manner. These digital assessments not only enhance creativity but also foster critical thinking and problem-solving skills.

Moreover, technology enables immediate feedback, which is essential for student growth. Online platforms can provide instant results and detailed feedback, allowing students to identify areas for improvement and take corrective actions promptly. This feedback loop empowers students to become self-directed learners, as they can track their progress and make informed decisions about their learning journey.

However, it is crucial for tech-savvy students to understand that assessment is not solely about grades. Assessment is a tool for learning, not just a measurement of performance. It provides students with opportunities to reflect on their strengths and weaknesses, set goals, and develop strategies for improvement. By embracing technology in the assessment process, students can actively engage in their learning, take ownership of their progress, and develop lifelong skills that extend beyond the classroom.

In conclusion, understanding the assessment process is vital for students seeking to master assessment with technology. By recognizing the purpose of assessment, embracing digital tools and platforms, and valuing feedback and self-reflection, students can leverage technology to enhance their learning experience. This subchapter aims to equip tech-savvy students with the knowledge and skills necessary to excel in assessment and evaluation, empowering them to become self-directed learners and thrive in the digital age.

Test-Taking Strategies for Technology-based Assessments

In today's digital age, technology has become an integral part of our educational system, including the way assessments are conducted. With the rise of online exams, it is crucial for tech-savvy students to develop effective test-taking strategies for technology-based assessments. This subchapter aims to equip students with the necessary skills to excel in these assessments.

One of the first things to consider when preparing for a technology-based assessment is familiarizing yourself with the testing platform. Take the time to explore the software or website where the exam will be conducted. Understand its features, functionalities, and layout. This will help you navigate through the platform more efficiently during the actual test, saving you precious time and reducing unnecessary stress.

Another important strategy is to practice using technology during your study sessions. Seek out online practice tests or quizzes that simulate the format and interface of the actual assessment. By doing so, you can become more comfortable with the technology and gain a better understanding of how to answer questions effectively within the given constraints.

Managing your time effectively is crucial in any test, but it becomes even more critical in technology-based assessments. Since these exams are often timed, it is essential to allocate your time wisely. Read the instructions carefully, plan your approach, and make sure to pace yourself throughout the exam. Keep an eye on the clock and prioritize the questions to ensure you complete the test within the given time frame.

Furthermore, it is important to remember that technology-based assessments often allow for review and revision of answers before submission. Take advantage of this feature by going back to review your answers, especially if you finish the test early. Proofread your responses, double-check calculations, and make any necessary corrections. However, be cautious not to second-guess yourself excessively, as this can lead to unnecessary mistakes.

Lastly, it is crucial to maintain a calm and focused mindset during the assessment. Distractions are prevalent when using technology, so find a quiet place, turn off notifications on your devices, and minimize any potential interruptions. Stay focused on the task at hand and trust in your preparation. Remember to breathe, take breaks if needed, and approach each question with confidence.

By implementing these test-taking strategies for technology-based assessments, you can enhance your performance and achieve better results. As a tech-savvy student, mastering the art of taking tests in a digital environment is an invaluable skill that will serve you well throughout your educational journey.

Chapter 4: Mastering Technology-based Test Formats

Multiple Choice Questions (MCQs)

Multiple Choice Questions (MCQs) are a popular form of assessment that can effectively measure your understanding and knowledge on various subjects. This subchapter will explore the benefits of MCQs and provide you with tips on how to approach them effectively.

MCQs offer several advantages over other assessment methods. Firstly, they provide a structured format that allows for quick and efficient grading, saving both your time and that of your teachers. Additionally, MCQs offer a standardized approach to assessment, ensuring fairness and consistency among all students. They also have the potential to cover a wide range of topics, making them suitable for testing your overall understanding of a subject.

To excel in MCQ assessments, it is essential to adopt a strategic approach. Start by carefully reading the question and all the available options before selecting an answer. Often, there may be more than one plausible choice, but your task is to identify the most accurate one. To do this, pay attention to keywords and phrases that can provide hints or context. Eliminate any options that you know are incorrect, and then choose the best remaining option.

Time management is crucial when dealing with MCQs. Since these questions are typically timed, it is essential to allocate an appropriate amount of time to each question. If you are unsure about an answer, make an educated guess and move on. Remember, leaving a question unanswered will guarantee a wrong answer, while guessing provides a chance of getting it right.

Preparing for MCQs involves a combination of subject knowledge and test-taking strategies. Review your course materials thoroughly, paying special attention to key concepts and terminology. Practice with sample MCQs to familiarize yourself with the format and identify areas where you may need additional study.

Finally, it is important to stay calm and focused during the test. Avoid second-guessing yourself or changing answers unless you have a good reason to do so. Trust your preparation and rely on your critical thinking skills to make the best choices.

In conclusion, MCQs offer an efficient and standardized way to assess your understanding and knowledge. By adopting a strategic approach and practicing with sample questions, you can excel in MCQ assessments and demonstrate your mastery of various subjects. Remember, preparation and confidence are key to achieving success in these assessments.

Fill in the Blanks

Assessment and evaluation are crucial aspects of education that determine our progress and understanding of various subjects. Traditional methods of assessment, such as written exams and quizzes, have been the norm for decades. However, with the advent of technology, students now have the opportunity to explore new and innovative ways to showcase their knowledge and skills. In this subchapter titled "Fill in the Blanks," we will delve into the world of technology-assisted assessment and how it can revolutionize the way students approach evaluations.

The fill in the blanks method of assessment has long been used as a tool to test comprehension and recall. In the past, it was limited to pen and paper, but now technology has made it even more interactive and engaging. With the help of various digital tools and platforms, students can now complete fill in the blank exercises online, providing an instant feedback loop to enhance their learning experience.

One of the primary advantages of using technology for fill in the blanks assessments is the ability to customize the difficulty level and content. Students can be presented with a range of questions, from simple recall to complex application-based scenarios. This allows for a personalized learning experience, catering to each student's unique strengths and weaknesses.

Furthermore, technology-assisted fill in the blanks assessments can provide immediate feedback, eliminating the long wait for teachers to grade and return papers. Real-time feedback enables students to identify their mistakes instantly and make corrections, thereby accelerating their learning process.

Another advantage of technology in fill in the blanks assessments is the ability to track progress. Students can keep a record of their performance over time, allowing them to identify patterns and areas that require further improvement. This data-driven approach empowers students to take control of their learning journey and set goals for themselves.

However, it is essential to remember that technology is not a substitute for critical thinking and understanding. While fill in the blanks assessments can be an effective tool, they should be used in conjunction with other forms of evaluation to provide a holistic view of a student's knowledge and skills.

In conclusion, the fill in the blanks method of assessment has evolved with the integration of technology. Students now have the opportunity to engage with interactive platforms that offer personalized learning experiences, instant feedback, and progress tracking. By embracing technology, students can enhance their assessment skills and master various subjects in an efficient and engaging manner.

True or False Questions

In the world of education, assessments play a crucial role in measuring students' understanding and knowledge. One commonly used assessment method is the true or false questions. These questions are designed to test your comprehension and critical thinking skills, making them an important tool for both teachers and students. In this subchapter, we will explore the significance of true or false questions in assessment and how you can effectively tackle them.

True or false questions are straightforward and require you to determine if a statement is true or false. They are often used to evaluate basic concepts and factual knowledge. However, do not underestimate their importance, as they can also assess your ability to analyze information and apply it to real-life situations.

One of the benefits of true or false questions is that they cover a wide range of topics, allowing teachers to assess various aspects of your understanding. These questions can test your memory recall, understanding of concepts, and ability to identify incorrect information. By answering these questions, you can demonstrate your knowledge and show how well you have grasped the material.

To effectively tackle true or false questions, it is essential to carefully read and analyze each statement. Look for keywords or phrases that might indicate whether the statement is true or false. Consider the context and think about any exceptions or conditions that might apply to the statement. Remember, even a single word can completely change the meaning of a statement, so pay close attention to details.

When answering true or false questions, avoid making assumptions or jumping to conclusions. Instead, base your response on evidence and reasoning. If you are unsure about the correctness of a statement, do not leave it blank. Take an educated guess by eliminating obviously incorrect options. Your educated guess might increase your chances of getting the answer right.

Lastly, it is crucial to manage your time effectively during assessments. True or false questions are often part of larger exams, so allocate your time wisely. Do not spend too much time on a single question, as it might hinder your progress on other sections.

In conclusion, true or false questions are an essential component of assessments in education. By understanding their significance and employing effective strategies, you can excel in tackling these questions and demonstrate your knowledge and understanding in various subject areas.

Matching Questions

Matching questions are a popular type of assessment tool used by educators to test students' knowledge and understanding. These questions require students to match items from two columns, usually by drawing lines or connecting them with arrows. This subchapter will discuss the benefits of matching questions and provide tips on how to excel in this type of assessment.

Matching questions offer several advantages for both educators and students. For educators, they are easy to create and score, saving valuable time and effort. They also provide a clear measure of students' comprehension of key concepts and their ability to make connections between related terms or ideas. Additionally, matching questions can be used to assess both factual knowledge and critical thinking skills, making them versatile for various subjects and grade levels.

For students, matching questions can be a helpful study tool. By organizing and connecting terms or concepts, students can reinforce their understanding of the material and improve their memory retention. Furthermore, these questions encourage students to think critically and make logical connections, enhancing their problem-solving abilities. Mastering matching questions can also boost students' confidence and reduce test anxiety, as they provide a clear format and structure.

To excel in matching questions, students should adopt effective strategies. First, it is crucial to carefully read and understand the instructions before starting the task. Pay attention to any limitations, such as using items only once or not at all. Next, scan both columns to get an overall sense of the available options. This initial survey will help identify any obvious matches or relationships.

When matching items, start with those that you are confident about. This will give you a solid foundation and build momentum. As you progress, be cautious about potential distractors and traps that may confuse you. Remember to double-check your answers before finalizing them.

To enhance your performance, practice is key. Seek out sample matching questions or create your own to reinforce your understanding of the material. Work on developing a systematic approach, such as organizing items by themes or categories, to help streamline your thought process during the assessment.

In conclusion, matching questions are a valuable assessment tool that allows educators to gauge students' comprehension and critical thinking abilities. For students, mastering matching questions can enhance their understanding, retention, and problem-solving skills. By implementing effective strategies and practicing regularly, students can excel in matching questions and achieve success in their academic assessments.

Short Answer Questions

In the realm of assessment and evaluation in education, short answer questions play a crucial role in measuring students' understanding of a subject matter. These questions require students to provide concise and specific responses, demonstrating their knowledge, critical thinking skills, and ability to communicate effectively.

Short answer questions are different from multiple-choice or true/false questions as they demand a deeper level of understanding and analysis. While multiple-choice questions may offer clues or options to choose from, short answer questions require students to recall information from memory and articulate their thoughts in a coherent manner.

To excel in answering short answer questions, students should follow a few key strategies. First and foremost, it is essential to read the question carefully and ensure a clear understanding of what is being asked. Pay attention to any specific instructions or requirements, such as a word limit or the need to provide examples.

Next, take some time to organize your thoughts before writing your response. Consider the main points that need to be addressed and create a brief outline. This will help you stay focused and ensure that you cover all the necessary information.

When writing your answer, be concise and to the point. Avoid unnecessary fluff or lengthy explanations that may distract from your main message. Instead, prioritize clarity and coherence, ensuring that your response is easy to understand and flows logically.

It is also important to provide evidence or examples to support your answer whenever possible. This helps to demonstrate a deeper understanding of the topic and adds credibility to your response. However, be mindful of the word limit and use examples sparingly, focusing on quality rather than quantity.

Lastly, before submitting your answer, take a few minutes to review and revise your response. Check for any spelling or grammatical errors and ensure that your answer fully addresses the question. This final step can greatly enhance the overall quality of your response.

Short answer questions can be challenging, but with practice and the right approach, students can effectively showcase their knowledge and analytical skills. By following these strategies, you will be better equipped to tackle short answer questions and achieve success in your assessments.

Essay Questions

Essay questions are a common form of assessment in education that require students to demonstrate their understanding of a particular topic or concept through written responses. These questions are designed to test students' critical thinking skills, analytical abilities, and ability to articulate their thoughts and ideas effectively.

When faced with an essay question, it is important for students to approach it strategically to ensure success. Here are some key tips to keep in mind when tackling essay questions:

1. Understand the question: Read the question carefully and make sure you fully understand what is being asked. Pay attention to keywords and phrases that indicate the specific task or requirements.

2. Plan your response: Before diving into the writing process, take a few minutes to brainstorm and outline your ideas. This will help you organize your thoughts and ensure that your essay has a clear structure.

3. Analyze and interpret: Essay questions often require students to analyze and interpret information or concepts. Take the time to think critically about the topic and provide evidence to support your arguments or claims.

4. Be concise and coherent: While it is essential to provide thorough and detailed responses, it is equally important to be concise and coherent in your writing. Avoid unnecessary repetition or going off-topic.

5. Use proper formatting and citations: Follow the guidelines provided by your instructor for formatting your essay. Additionally, if you are

referencing external sources, make sure to cite them properly to avoid plagiarism.

6. Revise and edit: After completing your essay, take the time to revise and edit your work. Check for grammatical errors, clarity of ideas, and overall coherence. It is also helpful to have someone else review your essay for feedback and suggestions.

Essay questions can be challenging, but with proper preparation and practice, you can excel in this form of assessment. Remember to approach each question with a clear understanding of what is being asked, and take the time to plan and structure your response effectively. By showcasing your critical thinking skills and providing well-supported arguments, you will demonstrate your mastery of the subject matter and impress your instructors.

Interactive Assessments

In today's digital age, technology has become an integral part of our lives, transforming the way we learn and communicate. As tech-savvy students, we have the unique advantage of harnessing the power of technology to enhance our educational experience, especially when it comes to assessment and evaluation in education.

This subchapter aims to explore the concept of interactive assessments and how they can revolutionize the way we demonstrate our knowledge and skills. Interactive assessments refer to the use of technology to engage students actively in the evaluation process, providing a more dynamic and personalized approach to learning.

One of the key benefits of interactive assessments is their ability to cater to diverse learning styles. Traditional assessments, such as written exams or essays, may not effectively capture the full potential of every student. However, with interactive assessments, we can utilize multimedia tools, such as videos, audio recordings, and interactive quizzes, to present information in various formats. This allows us to express our understanding in a way that resonates with our specific learning preferences, maximizing our ability to showcase our knowledge.

Furthermore, interactive assessments enable instant feedback, which is crucial for our growth and improvement. With traditional assessments, we often have to wait for days or even weeks to receive our results, making it challenging to identify areas of weakness or areas where we excelled. However, with technology-driven assessments, we can receive immediate feedback, allowing us to reflect on our performance in real-time and make necessary adjustments to our learning strategies.

Additionally, interactive assessments encourage collaboration and teamwork. Through online platforms and tools, we can engage in group projects, virtual discussions, and peer evaluations. These collaborative assessments not only enhance our understanding of the subject matter but also foster our ability to work effectively in teams, a vital skill in today's interconnected world.

It is important to note that while interactive assessments offer numerous advantages, they should not replace traditional assessments entirely. Instead, they should be integrated into our educational system to create a balanced and comprehensive evaluation approach. By embracing technology and incorporating interactive assessments into our learning journey, we can become more actively involved in our education, enhance our understanding, and develop the skills necessary for success in the digital age.

In conclusion, interactive assessments are a game-changer in the field of assessment and evaluation in education. As tech-savvy students, we have the opportunity to leverage technology to showcase our knowledge, receive immediate feedback, and collaborate with our peers. By embracing interactive assessments, we can transform our educational experience, becoming more engaged, adaptable, and prepared for the challenges that lie ahead.

Chapter 5: Maximizing the Potential of Technology-based Assessments

Utilizing Multimedia in Assessments

In today's digital age, technology has revolutionized the way we learn and communicate. As students, you are already familiar with the power and versatility of multimedia in your everyday lives. From watching videos online to creating presentations, multimedia has become an integral part of your educational experience. But did you know that it can also play a significant role in assessments?

Multimedia assessments offer a dynamic and interactive way to evaluate your knowledge and skills. Gone are the days of traditional paper-and-pencil exams that only test your ability to regurgitate information. With multimedia assessments, you have the opportunity to showcase your understanding through a variety of mediums, including videos, audio recordings, images, and interactive presentations.

One of the key advantages of utilizing multimedia in assessments is the ability to demonstrate your creativity and critical thinking skills. Instead of being limited to written responses, you can use visuals, audio, and even animations to express your ideas. For example, if you are asked to explain a complex concept, you can create a video tutorial that breaks it down in a visually appealing and engaging manner. This not only demonstrates your understanding but also allows you to communicate your ideas in a way that is unique to you.

Furthermore, multimedia assessments provide a more authentic and real-world experience. In today's workforce, employers are increasingly looking for candidates who can effectively communicate and present information using multimedia tools. By incorporating multimedia into your assessments, you are developing the skills that are highly valued in the professional world.

Additionally, multimedia assessments can be a great tool for self-reflection and self-assessment. When you create a multimedia project, you have the opportunity to review and evaluate your own work. This process allows you to identify areas of strength and areas for improvement, ultimately helping you to become a more self-directed learner.

However, it's important to note that utilizing multimedia in assessments also requires a certain level of digital literacy. It's crucial to familiarize yourself with various multimedia tools and platforms to effectively create and present your work. Take advantage of the resources available to you, such as tutorials and workshops, to enhance your multimedia skills.

In conclusion, the integration of multimedia in assessments offers numerous benefits for students like you. It allows you to showcase your creativity, critical thinking skills, and ability to effectively communicate information. Moreover, it provides a more authentic and real-world experience that aligns with the expectations of the modern workforce. Embrace the opportunities presented by multimedia assessments and continue to develop your digital literacy skills.

Collaborative Assessments using Technology

In today's digital age, technology has become an integral part of our lives, transforming the way we communicate, work, and learn. As students, you are at the forefront of this technological revolution, harnessing its potential to enhance your educational experience. One area where technology has had a significant impact is assessments, allowing for collaborative and interactive evaluation processes. This subchapter explores the concept of collaborative assessments using technology and how it can revolutionize the way you learn and demonstrate your knowledge.

Collaborative assessments involve students working together in teams, combining their skills, knowledge, and perspectives to solve problems or complete tasks. Traditionally, assessments were seen as individual tasks, with students working in isolation to showcase their understanding. However, with the advent of technology, collaborative assessments have become more accessible and efficient.

Technology offers a myriad of tools and platforms that enable students to collaborate seamlessly, regardless of their physical location. Virtual classrooms, online discussion boards, and video conferencing applications provide opportunities for real-time collaboration, allowing you to engage with your peers, share ideas, and receive instant feedback. These collaborative tools foster a sense of teamwork and promote critical thinking and communication skills.

Additionally, technology allows for the creation of multimedia projects, where students can work together to produce videos, podcasts, or interactive presentations. These projects not only assess your understanding of the subject matter but also encourage creativity, innovation, and problem-solving. By collaborating with your peers, you can tap into a diverse range of skills and perspectives, leading to a richer and more comprehensive final product.

Furthermore, technology enables the integration of formative assessments into the learning process. Formative assessments are ongoing evaluations that provide feedback and help identify areas for improvement. Through online quizzes, self-assessment tools, and interactive simulations, you can assess your knowledge and receive immediate feedback. Collaborative formative assessments also allow you to learn from your peers' strengths and weaknesses, fostering a supportive learning environment.

In conclusion, collaborative assessments using technology have revolutionized the traditional assessment methods, offering students new opportunities for learning and evaluation. By leveraging technology tools and platforms, you can engage in real-time collaboration, create multimedia projects, and integrate formative assessments into your learning journey. Embrace the power of technology and join the ranks of tech-savvy students who are mastering assessment with technology.

Incorporating Gamification Elements in Assessments

Incorporating Gamification Elements in Assessments: Making Learning Fun and Engaging for Tech-Savvy Students

Introduction:

In today's rapidly evolving digital world, technology has become an integral part of education. Students, with their innate tech-savviness, are constantly seeking interactive and engaging learning experiences. As a result, educators are finding innovative ways to incorporate gamification elements in assessments to make learning fun, interactive, and meaningful.

1. What is Gamification? Gamification is the process of applying game-design elements and principles to non-game contexts, such as education. It involves the use of game mechanics, such as points, levels, badges, and leaderboards, to motivate and engage students in their learning journey.

2. Benefits of Gamification in Assessments:
a) Increased Motivation: Gamification elements provide students with clear goals and rewards, making assessments more enjoyable and motivating.
b) Active Learning: Gamified assessments encourage students to take an active role in their own learning process, fostering critical thinking and problem-solving skills.
c) Personalized Learning: Gamification allows for adaptive assessments, where students receive individualized feedback based on their performance, enabling targeted improvement.
d) Immediate Feedback: Real-time feedback in gamified assessments helps students identify areas of strengths and weaknesses, enabling them to adjust their learning strategies accordingly.

3. Gamification Techniques in Assessments:
a) Badges and Achievements: Awarding badges and achievements for completing tasks or reaching milestones can motivate students to excel in their assessments.
b) Leaderboards and Competition: Introducing leaderboards can create healthy competition among students, driving them to perform better and achieve higher scores.
c) Leveling Up: Dividing assessments into levels or stages can provide a sense of progression and accomplishment, encouraging students to advance in their learning journey.
d) Storytelling and Narrative: Incorporating narratives and storytelling elements in assessments can immerse students in a captivating learning experience, making assessments more engaging and memorable.

Conclusion:
Incorporating gamification elements in assessments is a powerful way to harness the potential of technology and create a dynamic learning environment for tech-savvy students. By transforming assessments into interactive and engaging experiences, educators can motivate students, foster critical thinking skills, and enhance the overall learning process. As technology continues to evolve, the integration of gamification in assessments will undoubtedly play a significant role in shaping the future of education. So, embrace the gamified assessments and embark on a fun-filled learning adventure!

Personalizing Assessments with Adaptive Technology

In today's ever-evolving digital age, technology has become an integral part of our lives, including the realm of education. With the advent of adaptive technology, the landscape of assessment and evaluation in education has undergone a tremendous transformation. This subchapter aims to explore the concept of personalizing assessments through the integration of adaptive technology, specifically tailored for tech-savvy students like yourselves.

Adaptive technology refers to the use of intelligent algorithms and machine learning to customize assessments according to individual students' needs, strengths, and weaknesses. It takes into account your unique learning style, pace, and preferences to provide a personalized assessment experience. Gone are the days of one-size-fits-all tests that fail to capture your true abilities and potential.

One of the key advantages of adaptive technology is its ability to offer immediate feedback. Traditional assessments often had delayed feedback, leaving you uncertain about your performance. With adaptive technology, you receive instant feedback, allowing you to identify areas of improvement and make necessary adjustments in real-time. This ensures a continuous learning process, where you can build upon your strengths and work on your weaknesses efficiently.

Moreover, adaptive technology enables you to take control of your own learning journey. It empowers you to set personalized goals and track your progress effectively. By providing insights into your performance and highlighting areas that require attention, adaptive technology helps you take ownership of your education. You become an active participant in the assessment process, fostering a sense of autonomy and self-motivation.

Additionally, adaptive technology promotes engagement and motivation in your learning experience. Traditional assessments often lack the element of excitement and fail to capture your interest. However, with adaptive technology, assessments can be gamified, making them interactive and enjoyable. Through game-like elements such as badges, levels, and rewards, adaptive technology transforms assessments into a captivating experience, encouraging you to put forth your best effort and achieve optimal outcomes.

In conclusion, the integration of adaptive technology in assessments has revolutionized the field of assessment and evaluation in education. It personalizes the learning experience, providing you with tailored assessments that align with your individual needs and preferences. By offering immediate feedback, promoting self-directed learning, and enhancing engagement, adaptive technology empowers you to unlock your full potential and excel academically. Embrace the power of adaptive technology, and embark on a transformative journey towards mastering assessment with technology.

Analyzing Assessment Data for Self-Improvement

In today's tech-savvy world, students have the opportunity to leverage technology for their own self-improvement and academic success. Assessment data, collected through various tools and platforms, can be a goldmine of information that allows students to identify their strengths, weaknesses, and areas of improvement. In this subchapter, we will explore how students can effectively analyze assessment data to enhance their learning experience and achieve their goals.

Assessment and evaluation in education play a crucial role in determining a student's progress and understanding of a subject matter. However, it is not enough to simply receive a grade or feedback on an assignment or exam. To truly excel, students must take an active role in analyzing their assessment data and using it as a tool for self-improvement.

One of the first steps in analyzing assessment data is to review the feedback provided by teachers or instructors. This feedback often highlights areas where students can improve and provides valuable insights on their performance. By carefully reviewing this feedback, students can identify recurring patterns or areas of weakness that require additional attention.

In addition to teacher feedback, students can also utilize technology tools to analyze their assessment data. Online platforms and software can generate detailed reports and visualizations that provide a comprehensive overview of their performance. These reports can include information such as grade distribution, average scores, and comparisons with peers. By studying these reports, students can gain a deeper understanding of their strengths and weaknesses compared to their classmates, allowing them to set realistic goals for self-improvement.

Furthermore, technology can also help students track their progress over time. By using digital tools to record and analyze assessment data, students can identify trends and patterns in their performance. For example, they may notice that their scores tend to be higher during certain times of the day or week, suggesting the importance of scheduling study sessions accordingly.

Analyzing assessment data for self-improvement is not a one-time task but rather an ongoing process. By regularly reviewing their assessment data and making adjustments to their study strategies, students can continuously enhance their learning experience and achieve better results.

In conclusion, the ability to analyze assessment data is a valuable skill for students in today's digital age. By leveraging technology tools and platforms, students can gain insights into their strengths, weaknesses, and areas of improvement. By actively engaging with their assessment data, students can take control of their learning journey and make informed decisions to enhance their academic success. Remember, every assessment is an opportunity for growth, and analyzing the data it provides is the key to unlocking your full potential.

Chapter 6: Overcoming Challenges in Technology-based Assessments

Technical Issues and Troubleshooting

In today's digital age, technology has become an integral part of our lives, including our educational journey. As students, we rely heavily on technology for various aspects of our education, from research and collaboration to assessment and evaluation. However, it's not uncommon to encounter technical issues that can disrupt our learning experience. In this subchapter, we will explore some common technical issues that students may face and provide troubleshooting tips to overcome them.

One of the most common technical issues is connectivity problems. Internet connectivity, especially in schools or colleges with a large number of users, can be unstable or slow at times. If you find yourself facing connectivity issues, try restarting your device or connecting to a different Wi-Fi network. Additionally, make sure that your device's operating system and apps are up to date, as outdated software can also hinder connectivity.

Another common issue is software or app glitches. It can be frustrating when the tools we rely on for assessments or evaluations suddenly stop working or behave unexpectedly. In such cases, try closing and reopening the software or app, clearing cache and cookies, or reinstalling the program. If the issue persists, reach out to your instructor or the technical support team for further assistance.

Hardware malfunctions can also disrupt our learning process. Whether it's a malfunctioning keyboard, a frozen screen, or a battery that drains too quickly, hardware issues can be a major hindrance. If you encounter hardware problems, check if there are any software updates available for your device. Sometimes, an outdated software can cause hardware malfunctions. If the issue persists, consult a technician or the IT department of your institution.

Being proactive in preventing technical issues is equally important. Regularly backing up your important files and documents can save you from potential data loss. Additionally, maintaining good digital hygiene, such as running regular virus scans and avoiding suspicious websites or downloads, can prevent malware or other security-related issues.

In conclusion, as tech-savvy students navigating the world of assessment and evaluation, it is essential to be prepared for technical issues that may arise. By following the troubleshooting tips mentioned above and adopting proactive measures, you can minimize disruptions to your learning experience. Remember, technology is a powerful tool, and with the right skills and knowledge, you can overcome any technical challenge that comes your way.

Internet Connectivity and Reliability

In today's digital age, internet connectivity has become an integral part of our lives, especially for students. With the advent of technology, the way we learn and assess our knowledge has drastically changed. The internet has opened up a world of opportunities, allowing students to access vast amounts of information at the click of a button. However, it is crucial to understand the importance of internet connectivity and its reliability in the context of assessment and evaluation in education.

Internet connectivity refers to the ability to access and connect to the internet. It allows students to research, collaborate, and communicate with others, ultimately enhancing their learning experience. With a reliable internet connection, students can access online resources, participate in virtual classrooms, and engage in discussions with peers and instructors. This connectivity also enables students to submit assignments and take online assessments, providing flexibility and convenience.

Reliability is another key aspect of internet connectivity. A reliable internet connection ensures that students can access the internet consistently without interruptions or disruptions. It is essential for seamless communication, uninterrupted online assessments, and real-time collaboration. Unreliable connections can lead to frustration, lost productivity, and even incomplete assessments, negatively impacting the learning process.

As students, it is crucial to be aware of the factors that can affect internet connectivity and reliability. Factors such as distance from the Wi-Fi router, network congestion, and the quality of the internet service provider can all impact the reliability of the internet connection. It is advisable to ensure a strong Wi-Fi signal, use a reliable internet service provider, and be mindful of the number of devices connected to the network to maintain a stable internet connection.

To overcome challenges related to internet connectivity and reliability, students can employ various strategies. It is important to have a backup plan in case of internet outages, such as using a mobile hotspot or accessing public Wi-Fi. Additionally, downloading necessary resources in advance can ensure access to essential materials even without an internet connection.

In conclusion, internet connectivity and reliability play a crucial role in assessment and evaluation in education. Students must understand the significance of a stable and reliable internet connection in enhancing their learning experience. By being proactive and prepared, students can overcome challenges related to connectivity issues and ensure a smooth assessment process. Embracing technology and harnessing the power of the internet can truly empower tech-savvy students in mastering assessment with technology.

Addressing Security and Privacy Concerns

In this digital age, where technology plays a significant role in education, it is crucial for students to be aware of the security and privacy concerns that come with using technology for assessment and evaluation. While technology offers numerous benefits, it is important to understand how to protect personal information and maintain a safe and secure learning environment. This subchapter aims to provide you, as tech-savvy students, with essential knowledge and strategies to address these concerns effectively.

First and foremost, it is essential to understand the importance of protecting your personal information. When using technology for assessments, be cautious about sharing sensitive data, such as your full name, address, or phone number, unless explicitly required by the assessment. Always be mindful of the platforms and applications you use, ensuring they have proper security measures in place to safeguard your information. Additionally, regularly update your passwords and avoid sharing them with anyone to prevent unauthorized access.

Another significant concern is ensuring the privacy of your assessment data. When utilizing digital platforms, make sure you are familiar with their privacy policies and terms of service. It is crucial to choose platforms that prioritize data security and do not sell or share your information with third parties. If you have any doubts about a platform's privacy practices, consult with your teacher or school administrator to find a suitable alternative.

Additionally, familiarize yourself with digital ethics and responsible use of technology. Avoid engaging in any form of cyberbullying, cheating, or unethical behavior when using technology for assessments. Respect the privacy and intellectual property rights of others, including your classmates and teachers, by not sharing or distributing assessment content without proper authorization.

Lastly, remember that security and privacy are not solely the responsibility of educators and administrators. As tech-savvy students, it is crucial that you actively contribute to maintaining a safe and secure learning environment. Report any security or privacy concerns you encounter to your teacher or school authorities, as they can address these issues promptly and ensure the protection of all students.

By being aware of security and privacy concerns and adopting responsible digital practices, you can confidently navigate the world of technology in assessments. Remember, technology is a powerful tool that can enhance your learning experience, but it is essential to prioritize your safety and privacy while utilizing it for educational purposes.

Dealing with Distractions and Time Management

In today's fast-paced digital age, students face an unprecedented number of distractions that can hinder their ability to focus and manage their time effectively. From social media notifications to endless streams of online content, it can be challenging to stay on track and prioritize academic tasks. However, by adopting effective strategies for dealing with distractions and honing their time management skills, tech-savvy students can pave their way to success in assessment and evaluation in education.

One crucial aspect of dealing with distractions is recognizing the impact they have on productivity. Constant interruptions can disrupt the flow of concentration and make it difficult to retain information or complete tasks efficiently. To combat this, students should consider implementing techniques such as the Pomodoro Technique. Based on the idea of working in short, focused bursts, this method involves setting a timer for 25 minutes and dedicating that time solely to the task at hand. After each Pomodoro, take a short break of 5 minutes, and after completing four Pomodoros, take a more extended break of 15-30 minutes. This approach not only helps manage distractions but also enhances productivity by promoting regular breaks and maintaining a healthy work-life balance.

Another essential aspect of effective time management is setting clear goals and creating a structured schedule. By breaking down larger tasks into smaller, manageable steps, students can tackle their workload systematically and prevent feeling overwhelmed. Digital tools such as task management apps or online calendars can be invaluable in organizing deadlines and prioritizing assignments. Additionally, creating a to-do list at the start of the day or week can provide a visual representation of the tasks that need to be completed, helping students stay focused and motivated.

Furthermore, it is crucial to establish a conducive study environment that minimizes distractions. Find a quiet space free from noise and other disruptions, and consider using productivity-boosting apps or browser extensions that block access to distracting websites or limit the use of social media during study sessions. Additionally, practicing self-discipline by setting boundaries and avoiding multitasking can significantly improve concentration and overall productivity.

Ultimately, mastering the art of dealing with distractions and time management is essential for tech-savvy students aiming to excel in assessment and evaluation in education. By implementing strategies such as the Pomodoro Technique, setting clear goals, and creating a structured schedule, students can optimize their productivity and achieve their academic goals. Embracing these techniques will not only lead to success in assessments but also equip students with valuable skills for their future endeavors.

Chapter 7: Tips for Success in Technology-based Assessments

Developing Effective Study Habits

In today's fast-paced world, students face numerous challenges in their academic journey. With the advent of technology, students are now expected to be tech-savvy while also excelling in their assessments. To achieve success in this digital age, it is crucial for students to develop effective study habits that harness the power of technology. This subchapter aims to guide students on how to master assessment using technology by cultivating efficient study habits.

The first step towards developing effective study habits is to create a conducive learning environment. Find a quiet space free from distractions where you can focus solely on your studies. Ensure that you have all the necessary tech tools, such as a laptop or tablet, internet access, and relevant software or applications. Organize your study materials, whether they are digital or physical, so that you can easily access them when needed.

Next, utilize technology to enhance your learning experience. Take advantage of online resources, such as e-books, educational websites, and interactive platforms, to supplement your studies. Use productivity apps and tools to manage your time effectively and set goals for each study session. Collaborate with your peers through online platforms, such as discussion forums or study groups, to exchange ideas and gain different perspectives on the subject matter.

To maximize your study efforts, employ effective study techniques. One popular method is the Pomodoro Technique, which involves studying in short bursts of focused work followed by short breaks. Use digital flashcards or study apps to reinforce your knowledge and improve retention. Experiment with different note-taking techniques, such as mind maps or digital annotations, to find what works best for you.

Developing a consistent study routine is essential for long-term success. Set a schedule that includes dedicated study time, breaks, and leisure activities to maintain a healthy work-life balance. Be disciplined and committed to sticking to your study plan, while also allowing flexibility to adapt as needed.

Finally, regularly assess your progress and adjust your study habits accordingly. Use technology to track your performance, whether through online quizzes, self-assessment tools, or educational software. Analyze your strengths and weaknesses to identify areas for improvement and seek additional help or resources when necessary.

By developing effective study habits and harnessing the power of technology, you can become a tech-savvy student who excels in assessments. Embrace the digital tools and resources available to you, create a conducive learning environment, and cultivate a consistent study routine. Remember, mastering assessment with technology is not only about being proficient in using technology but also about leveraging it to enhance your learning and achieve academic success.

Managing Test Anxiety in Technology-based Assessments

Introduction:

In today's digital age, technology has revolutionized the way we learn and assess knowledge. With the advent of technology-based assessments, students are now faced with a new set of challenges, one of which is test anxiety. This subchapter aims to equip students with strategies to manage test anxiety specifically in technology-based assessments.

Understanding Test Anxiety:

Test anxiety is a common experience among students, characterized by feelings of fear, stress, and apprehension before or during an assessment. In technology-based assessments, this anxiety may be intensified due to factors such as unfamiliarity with the technology, time constraints, and fear of technical glitches. However, with the right mindset and preparation, students can overcome test anxiety and perform at their best.

Strategies to Manage Test Anxiety:

1. Familiarize Yourself with the Technology: Prior to the assessment, take time to familiarize yourself with the technology platform. Practice using the tools and features that will be used in the assessment. This will help reduce anxiety and increase your confidence during the actual test.

2. Create a Study Plan: Develop a study plan that incorporates practice tests or quizzes using the same technology you will encounter in the assessment. This will not only help you become more comfortable with the technology but also improve your familiarity with the content.

3. Practice Time Management: Time management is crucial in technology-based assessments. Develop strategies to pace yourself effectively, such as dividing the allotted time for each question or section. Practice timing yourself during practice assessments to build confidence and reduce anxiety about running out of time.

4. Develop Test-Taking Strategies: Explore different test-taking strategies that work for you. This may include reading all the questions first, answering easier questions first, or using process of elimination for multiple-choice questions. Having a plan in place will help you feel more in control during the assessment.

5. Practice Relaxation Techniques: Incorporate relaxation techniques, such as deep breathing, progressive muscle relaxation, or visualization exercises, into your test preparation routine. These techniques can help calm your mind and body, reducing test anxiety.

Conclusion:

Technology-based assessments offer unique challenges for students, including test anxiety. By familiarizing yourself with the technology, creating a study plan, practicing time management, developing test-taking strategies, and using relaxation techniques, you can effectively manage test anxiety and perform at your best. Remember, preparation and a positive mindset are key to overcoming test anxiety in technology-based assessments. Embrace the opportunities that technology brings to assessment and evaluation, and use these strategies to excel in your academic journey.

Time Management Strategies for Online Assessments

In today's digital age, technology has revolutionized the way we assess and evaluate students' knowledge and skills. Online assessments have become increasingly popular, providing students with the convenience and flexibility to complete assessments from anywhere at any time. However, with this convenience comes the challenge of managing your time effectively to ensure you perform your best. In this subchapter, we will discuss some time management strategies specifically tailored for online assessments.

Firstly, it is crucial to familiarize yourself with the assessment format and requirements well in advance. Understand the types of questions you will be asked, the time allotted for each section, and any specific guidelines or instructions. This will allow you to plan your time accordingly and allocate sufficient time for each task.

Creating a study schedule can greatly help you manage your time effectively. Break down your study sessions into smaller, manageable chunks and allocate specific time slots for each topic or subject. By doing so, you can ensure that you cover all the necessary material and avoid last-minute cramming. Stick to your schedule and avoid distractions during your study sessions to make the most of your time.

When it comes to online assessments, it is essential to have a reliable internet connection and a suitable device. Ensure that your device is fully charged, and you have all the necessary software or applications installed beforehand. Technical issues can eat up valuable time, so it is best to check your equipment and connection well in advance to avoid any last-minute surprises.

During the assessment, time management is key. Read the instructions carefully and allocate your time wisely for each question or task. If there are multiple-choice questions, quickly scan through the options and eliminate obviously incorrect answers to save time. For longer, essay-type questions, create a brief outline before you start writing to ensure coherence and a clear structure.

Lastly, do not forget to take breaks. Continuous studying or assessment-taking can lead to fatigue and decreased concentration. Schedule short breaks between study sessions or during long assessments to recharge your mind and maintain focus.

By implementing these time management strategies, you can optimize your performance in online assessments. Remember, effective time management not only helps you complete assessments successfully but also reduces stress and enhances your overall learning experience. Mastering the art of managing your time will equip you with a valuable skill that will benefit you not only during your academic journey but also in your future endeavors.

Seeking Support and Assistance when Needed

In the fast-paced world of technology, students today are expected to be tech-savvy and independent learners. However, it is important to remember that seeking support and assistance when needed is not a sign of weakness, but rather a crucial skill for success. This subchapter aims to emphasize the importance of reaching out for help and provide guidance on how to effectively seek support and assistance in the context of assessment and evaluation in education.

Assessment and evaluation can be challenging tasks, requiring a deep understanding of the subject matter and the ability to effectively demonstrate knowledge and skills. It is common for students to face difficulties and uncertainties during this process. Seeking support and assistance can help alleviate these challenges and ensure a more comprehensive learning experience.

One of the first steps in seeking support is recognizing the need for help. This can be achieved by reflecting on personal strengths and weaknesses, identifying areas of improvement, and acknowledging when additional guidance is required. It is crucial to understand that seeking assistance does not diminish one's abilities, but rather enhances them.

Once the need for support is established, students can explore various avenues to seek assistance. This may include approaching teachers, classmates, or online resources. Teachers are valuable resources who can provide guidance, clarify doubts, and offer constructive feedback. Building a positive and open relationship with teachers can greatly facilitate the learning process.

Classmates can also be a valuable source of support. Collaborative learning environments allow students to share insights, ask questions, and benefit from a collective knowledge pool. Engaging in group discussions and study groups can foster a supportive and enriching learning experience.

In today's digital age, online resources can also play a crucial role in seeking assistance. Online forums, educational websites, and tutorial videos can provide additional explanations, examples, and practice material. These resources are available 24/7, allowing students to seek assistance at their convenience.

Remember, seeking support and assistance is not a sign of weakness but rather a strength. It demonstrates a proactive approach to learning and a commitment to personal growth. By reaching out for help, students can enhance their understanding, improve their performance, and develop the necessary skills to become successful, tech-savvy learners.

In summary, this subchapter has emphasized the importance of seeking support and assistance when needed in the context of assessment and evaluation in education. It has highlighted the significance of recognizing the need for help, and provided guidance on how to effectively seek support from teachers, classmates, and online resources. By embracing the notion of seeking assistance, students can enhance their learning experience, overcome challenges, and ultimately achieve success in their academic endeavors.

Chapter 8: Exploring Future Trends in Technology-based Assessments

Artificial Intelligence and Machine Learning in Assessments

In this ever-evolving digital age, technology has made its way into almost every aspect of our lives, including education. With the rapid advancements in Artificial Intelligence (AI) and Machine Learning (ML), assessments have taken on a whole new level of efficiency and effectiveness. This subchapter aims to explore how AI and ML are transforming the field of assessment and evaluation in education for tech-savvy students like you.

One of the most significant advantages of AI and ML in assessments is the ability to provide personalized feedback. Traditional assessments often rely on standardized scoring systems, which may not capture the unique strengths and weaknesses of individual students. However, with AI-powered assessments, the technology can analyze your responses and provide tailored feedback based on your specific learning needs. This personalized approach not only helps you understand your areas of improvement but also enables you to focus your efforts on specific knowledge gaps.

Moreover, AI and ML can assist in creating adaptive assessments. These types of assessments adapt to your performance level and adjust the difficulty of the questions accordingly. This way, you are constantly challenged at an appropriate level, ensuring that the assessment accurately reflects your knowledge and abilities. Adaptive assessments also save time by eliminating irrelevant questions, allowing you to complete assessments more efficiently.

AI and ML also enable educators to analyze big data to gain insights into student performance trends. By analyzing vast amounts of assessment data, patterns and trends can be identified, helping educators make informed decisions regarding curriculum design, instruction, and intervention strategies. For you as a student, this means that assessments can be better aligned with your learning goals, ensuring that you receive a high-quality education tailored to your needs.

However, it is important to note that while AI and ML offer numerous benefits, they are not without limitations. AI algorithms may not always accurately capture the complexity of human thought processes, potentially resulting in biased assessments. It is crucial for both students and educators to be aware of these limitations and actively engage in discussions on ethical considerations in the use of AI and ML in assessments.

In conclusion, AI and ML have the potential to revolutionize assessments and evaluation in education. As a tech-savvy student, you have the opportunity to benefit from personalized feedback, adaptive assessments, and improved educational experiences. However, it is important to stay informed about the ethical implications of AI and ML and actively participate in shaping the future of technology in education.

Virtual Reality and Augmented Reality Assessments

In the rapidly evolving world of technology, it is not surprising that virtual reality (VR) and augmented reality (AR) have made their way into the realm of assessments and evaluations in education. These cutting-edge technologies offer students a unique and immersive learning experience that goes beyond traditional methods of assessment. This subchapter explores the potential of VR and AR in revolutionizing the way students are assessed.

Virtual reality assessments provide students with an opportunity to engage with content in a simulated environment. By donning a VR headset, students can step into virtual worlds that recreate real-life scenarios or offer simulations of complex concepts. This technology allows for interactive and experiential learning, enabling students to demonstrate their understanding of concepts in a more authentic manner. For example, in a science class, students can explore the human body from within or conduct virtual experiments in a safe and controlled environment. These activities not only enhance student engagement but also provide valuable data for assessment purposes.

On the other hand, augmented reality assessments merge the physical and digital worlds, overlaying virtual elements onto the real world. Through the use of smartphones or tablets, students can access AR applications that provide additional information, interactive features, or even gamified assessments. For instance, in a history class, students can use AR to scan historical artifacts and receive contextual information or engage in virtual tours of historical sites. These assessments promote active participation and critical thinking skills, as students are required to analyze and interpret the augmented content.

Both VR and AR assessments offer numerous advantages. They provide personalized and adaptive learning experiences that cater to individual student needs. These technologies can track and analyze student interactions, providing instant feedback and allowing for timely intervention. Furthermore, they can accommodate different learning styles, making assessments more inclusive and accessible for all students.

However, it is important to consider the limitations and ethical implications of using VR and AR assessments. Not all schools may have the necessary resources to implement these technologies, creating a potential digital divide among students. Moreover, issues related to privacy and data security need to be addressed to ensure student information is protected.

In conclusion, virtual reality and augmented reality assessments have the potential to revolutionize the field of assessment and evaluation in education. These technologies offer students a unique and immersive learning experience, promoting engagement, critical thinking, and personalized learning. While there are challenges to overcome, the benefits of incorporating VR and AR assessments are vast. As students, embracing these technologies can open up new opportunities for demonstrating knowledge and skills, preparing us for the tech-savvy world we live in.

Adaptive Assessments for Individualized Learning

Assessment and evaluation play a crucial role in education, helping students and educators understand progress, identify strengths and weaknesses, and make informed decisions for personalized learning. In today's digital age, technology has revolutionized the way we approach assessments, allowing for adaptive assessments that cater to the unique needs of each student. This subchapter explores the concept of adaptive assessments for individualized learning, providing insights into how technology can be harnessed to enhance the assessment process.

Adaptive assessments are designed to dynamically adjust to the knowledge and capabilities of an individual student. Unlike traditional assessments that follow a one-size-fits-all approach, adaptive assessments leverage technology to tailor questions, content, and difficulty levels based on the student's responses and performance. This personalized approach ensures that students are challenged at their appropriate level, promoting a deeper understanding of the material and fostering a sense of achievement.

One of the key advantages of adaptive assessments is their ability to identify gaps in knowledge or skills. By adapting the questions to match the student's proficiency, these assessments can pinpoint areas where a student may be struggling or excelling. This valuable data can then be used to guide instructional decisions, allowing educators to provide targeted interventions or enrichment activities that address the specific needs of each student.

Furthermore, adaptive assessments offer immediate feedback, allowing students to gauge their understanding and progress in real-time. This instant feedback not only reinforces learning but also empowers students to take ownership of their education. With access to detailed analytics and performance metrics, students can identify their strengths and weaknesses, set goals, and track their progress over time. This self-directed learning approach fosters a growth mindset, encouraging students to embrace challenges and persevere through difficulties.

Technology plays a vital role in facilitating adaptive assessments. With the abundance of digital tools and learning platforms available, students can engage in adaptive assessments anywhere, anytime. These platforms utilize algorithms that analyze student responses to generate tailored questions, ensuring a personalized learning experience. From interactive quizzes to game-based assessments, technology offers a wide range of engaging and immersive assessment formats, making the learning process more enjoyable and effective.

In conclusion, adaptive assessments for individualized learning have transformed the assessment and evaluation landscape in education. By harnessing technology, educators can create personalized learning experiences that cater to the unique needs and abilities of each student. Adaptive assessments provide valuable insights, immediate feedback, and promote self-directed learning, empowering students to take control of their education. As technology continues to advance, the possibilities for adaptive assessments are limitless, shaping the future of assessment and evaluation in education.

Blockchain Technology in Credentialing and Certification

In today's rapidly evolving digital landscape, blockchain technology has emerged as a powerful tool with the potential to revolutionize various industries. One area where blockchain is making a significant impact is in credentialing and certification. This subchapter aims to introduce students to the concept of blockchain technology and its potential implications in the field of assessment and evaluation in education.

Blockchain technology is a decentralized, transparent, and immutable ledger that records and verifies transactions across multiple computers. It gained prominence with the rise of cryptocurrencies like Bitcoin, but its applications extend far beyond digital currencies. Blockchain has the potential to transform the way credentials and certifications are verified and managed.

Traditionally, the process of verifying credentials and certifications has been time-consuming and prone to errors. Students often have to submit physical documents and rely on centralized authorities to verify their authenticity. However, blockchain technology offers a secure and efficient alternative. By storing credentials on a blockchain, students can have complete control over their records and share them with potential employers or educational institutions with ease.

One of the key advantages of using blockchain technology in credentialing is its ability to prevent fraud. Since the information stored on a blockchain cannot be altered or tampered with, employers and educational institutions can trust the validity of the credentials presented by students. This eliminates the need for time-consuming manual verification processes and reduces the risk of fraudulent claims.

Furthermore, blockchain technology enables the creation of smart contracts, which are self-executing contracts with predefined rules. These smart contracts can automate the verification and validation of credentials, streamlining the process for both students and institutions. Additionally, blockchain-based credentialing systems can provide real-time access to up-to-date information, ensuring that employers and educational institutions have the most accurate and relevant data about a student's qualifications.

As students in the field of assessment and evaluation in education, it is essential to understand the potential implications of blockchain technology on the future of credentialing and certification. By embracing this technology, students can take control of their educational achievements, reduce the risk of fraud, and simplify the verification process. It is crucial to stay informed about emerging technologies like blockchain and explore how they can enhance the assessment and evaluation processes in education.

In conclusion, blockchain technology has the potential to revolutionize the way credentials and certifications are managed and verified. By utilizing blockchain, students can have complete control over their records, prevent fraud, and simplify the verification process. As tech-savvy students in the field of assessment and evaluation in education, it is essential to explore the potential of blockchain technology and stay ahead in this rapidly changing digital world.

Chapter 9: Conclusion

Recap of Key Concepts

As we near the end of this book, it is important to take a moment and reflect upon the key concepts we have explored throughout our journey to become tech-savvy students mastering assessment with technology. These concepts have equipped us with the knowledge and skills necessary to navigate the ever-evolving landscape of assessment and evaluation in education.

First and foremost, we have learned about the importance of assessment and evaluation in our educational journey. Assessment is not merely a tool for grading or labeling students, but rather a means to measure our progress, identify areas of strength and weakness, and guide our learning. It provides valuable feedback that helps us grow and improve our skills.

We have also delved into the role of technology in assessment and evaluation. Technology has revolutionized the way we learn and are assessed. From online quizzes and digital portfolios to virtual simulations and adaptive learning platforms, technology offers new and innovative ways to assess our knowledge and abilities. It allows us to engage with interactive and personalized assessments that cater to our unique learning styles.

Throughout this book, we have explored various types of assessments, such as formative and summative assessments. Formative assessments provide ongoing feedback to guide our learning, while summative assessments measure our overall understanding of a topic. Both are essential in our educational journey and contribute to our growth as students.

Furthermore, we have discussed the significance of rubrics in assessment and evaluation. Rubrics provide clear criteria for evaluation, ensuring fairness and consistency in grading. They also empower us to take ownership of our learning by understanding the expectations and standards set for each assignment.

Finally, we have touched upon the importance of data-driven decision-making in assessment and evaluation. By analyzing and interpreting assessment data, we can identify patterns, trends, and areas of improvement. This data-driven approach enables us to make informed decisions about our learning and tailor our study strategies accordingly.

As tech-savvy students, we now possess the knowledge and skills to leverage technology in our assessment and evaluation processes. By embracing the concepts explored in this book, we can actively engage in our own learning journey, take control of our assessments, and maximize our potential for success.

So, as we conclude this subchapter, let us take a moment to appreciate the key concepts we have explored. Through assessment and evaluation, technology, various types of assessments, rubrics, and data-driven decision-making, we have laid the foundation for becoming successful, tech-savvy students mastering assessment with technology. May these concepts stay with us as we continue to grow and thrive in our educational endeavors.

Embracing Technology-based Assessments for Lifelong Learning

In today's rapidly evolving technological landscape, it is essential for students to embrace technology-based assessments as a means to enhance their lifelong learning journey. As the world becomes increasingly digital, the traditional methods of assessment are being revolutionized to accommodate the needs and expectations of tech-savvy students. This subchapter aims to explore the significance of technology-based assessments in the context of lifelong learning and its relevance to students in the field of assessment and evaluation in education.

Technology-based assessments offer students a dynamic and interactive learning experience, enabling them to showcase their knowledge and skills in a more engaging and authentic manner. Unlike traditional paper-based exams, technology-based assessments provide students with opportunities to apply their knowledge in real-world scenarios, fostering critical thinking, problem-solving, and creativity. By simulating real-life situations, these assessments equip students with the skills they need to succeed in their future careers.

Moreover, technology-based assessments provide students with immediate feedback, allowing them to identify their strengths and areas for improvement. This timely feedback helps students understand their progress and make necessary adjustments to enhance their learning. With the ability to receive personalized feedback, students can take ownership of their education and actively engage in self-reflection and self-improvement, promoting lifelong learning.

Furthermore, technology-based assessments offer students a platform to collaborate and communicate with their peers, fostering a sense of community and promoting social learning. Through online discussion forums, collaborative projects, and interactive assessments, students can exchange ideas, learn from one another's perspectives, and develop a deeper understanding of the subject matter. This collaborative learning environment enhances students' ability to work in teams, a crucial skill required for success in the professional world.

In conclusion, embracing technology-based assessments is essential for students in the field of assessment and evaluation in education. These assessments provide students with a dynamic and interactive learning experience, immediate feedback, and opportunities for collaboration. By harnessing the power of technology, students can enhance their lifelong learning journey, develop essential skills, and prepare themselves for a rapidly changing world. As tech-savvy students, it is crucial to embrace technology-based assessments and leverage their benefits to achieve personal and professional success.

Final Thoughts and Encouragement for Students in Mastering Assessment with Technology.

Final Thoughts and Encouragement for Students in Mastering Assessment with Technology

Congratulations on completing this journey towards mastering assessment with technology! Throughout this book, we have explored various ways in which technology can enhance your learning experience and help you excel in assessments. As you reach the end of this subchapter, we would like to leave you with some final thoughts and encouragement to keep pushing forward in your educational journey.

First and foremost, it is crucial to remember that technology is not a substitute for hard work and dedication. While it can undoubtedly enhance your learning experience, it is ultimately up to you to put in the effort and make the most out of the resources available to you. Embrace technology as a tool that can amplify your efforts and provide new opportunities for growth and achievement.

One of the key takeaways from this book is the importance of adaptability and being open to new ways of learning and assessment. As technology continues to advance at a rapid pace, it is essential to stay updated and embrace new tools and techniques that can optimize your learning experience. Don't be afraid to explore new apps, software, or online platforms that can help you better understand and demonstrate your knowledge.

Another important aspect to consider is the need for critical thinking and discernment when using technology for assessment purposes. While technology can provide instant feedback and automate certain processes, it is crucial to question and evaluate the validity and reliability of the tools you are using. Always strive for accuracy and ensure that technology is enhancing the assessment process rather than hindering it.

Lastly, we want to encourage you to never stop learning and seeking improvement. Mastering assessment with technology is an ongoing process, and there will always be new tools and strategies to explore. Take advantage of the resources available to you, such as online courses, webinars, and forums, to continue expanding your knowledge and skills in assessment and evaluation.

Remember, you have the power to shape your educational experience and use technology to your advantage. Embrace the opportunities it presents, but always stay true to your goals and work ethic. By mastering assessment with technology, you are equipping yourself with valuable skills that will benefit you not only in your academic journey but also in the professional world.

We wish you all the best in your future endeavors and hope that this book has provided you with the guidance and inspiration needed to excel in assessment and evaluation with the help of technology. Keep pushing forward, stay curious, and never stop learning!

9 798869 045959